## *Praise for Wholeheartedly*

Because Angela's thoughts speak clearly from her heart, this beautifully written book makes a convincing case for apostolic celibacy. There is truly unabashed conviction. She shows that celibacy needs to be nurtured by a robust friendship with Christ through acts of piety done with the heart. I say this because celibacy ceases to have experiential meaning when piety becomes reduced to routine devotions and there is an absence of apostolic zeal. This timely book, written with genuine conviction and honesty, must get into the hands of both young single men and women and married people. Five stars from me!

—Fr. Peter Armenio,
author of *Highlights of the Catholic Faith*

As I read Angela Fortunato's *Wholeheartedly*, one word kept popping into my mind—Joy! It is clear that this little book on apostolic celibacy was written by one who loves her vocation. And, of course, what's not to love when one is doing God's will?! I plan to give a copy of this book to my grandchildren when they come of age whether or not they are discerning a celibate vocation. We all need a better understanding of and appreciation for the gift of apostolic celibacy. This wonderful book will be an eye-opener for many.

—Stephen Gabriel, author of *Put Out into the Deep: Become the Apostle You are Called to Be*

As a very happily married member of Opus Dei, I have for decades been loved and cared for by a succession of fabulous women who have answered God's call to apostolic celibacy. I have prayed often and insistently for more such women, but almost always because I saw them as essential to *getting what I want*, namely, the growth and spread of Opus Dei to every corner of the world. In this book, Ms. Fortunato, with generosity and courage, opens up the intimate interior world of apostolic celibacy, giving me more than a hint of what God offers to the soul who answers such a call. Our Catholic culture needs this book, enriched and enlivened by the author's contemporary experiences, to broaden and deepen our understanding of this beautiful divine path.

—Dia Boyle, author of *The Thoughtful Home*

# Wholeheartedly

## GOD'S MYSTERY OF LOVE IN THE CALL TO CELIBACY

# Wholeheartedly

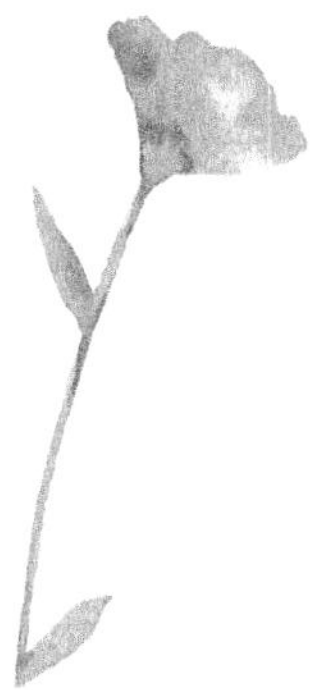

## GOD'S MYSTERY OF LOVE IN THE CALL TO CELIBACY

Angela T. Fortunato

Scepter

Published by Scepter Publishers, Inc.
info@scepterpublishers.org
www.scepterpublishers.org
800-322-8773
New York



Cover Image: Anastasia Lembrik
Cover Design by Rose Design
Text Design and Pagination by Rose Design

Paperback ISBN: 978-1-59417-529-9
eBook ISBN: 978-1-59417-530-5

Library of Congress Control Number: 2024944936

Printed in the United States of America

Dedicated to my sister on her thirtieth wedding anniversary.

In gratitude to my many brothers and sisters in Opus Dei
who have contributed to this story by their years of fidelity,
almost always without realizing it.

# CONTENTS

# INTRODUCTION

If you are accustomed to pondering God's mysteries, then this little book may be for you. The content mirrors what I discuss with teenage girls and their parents as the girls discern their paths toward God and with God. These chapters come from circumstances and events of my own life which include a myriad of uncitable conversations with spiritual guides, trusted friends, and loved ones. I share some personal insights and inspirations the Holy Spirit gave to me at different times in my life, meant to meet my particular timely need, with the hope that my experiences can help others. The few resources to which I refer are written texts that directly touch on this topic of apostolic celibacy. I say few because there are currently insufficient publications on the topic, most of which are not written in English, and almost all of which are written by priests. I am one of many, many women who could have written this book.

I share my ponderings on the vocation of apostolic celibacy as I celebrate the thirtieth anniversary of my "Damascus moment" (see Acts 22), when God knocked me off my proverbial horse. In the summer of 1993, I was a rising junior in a public high school in New Jersey. During that time, I worked part-time in a center of Opus Dei in New York City and attended monthly days of recollection for high school girls. This is when I first sensed my call to apostolic celibacy, the call to embrace the lifelong commitment to the single life in service of Christ's Church. Not coincidentally, during that summer countless Christians prayed for young people in the United States, in anticipation of Pope John Paul II's visit with the youth. I was one beneficiary of those prayers, as I joined the pope at Mile High Stadium in Denver for World Youth Day. St. John Paul has been a prominent figure throughout my vocational journey, and his *Theology of the Body* is one of the few written resources that provided answers to my many questions about the value of apostolic celibacy in this world.

Although I first sensed my calling in high school, it was not until my freshman year of college that I made any sort of commitment.[1] I did so on my eighteenth birthday, which is the youngest age that the Church allows anyone to make a vocational commitment. On that day, I attended Mass in the old Giants Stadium in New Jersey with, once again, my beloved Pope John Paul II. It was a truly remarkable birthday, and not solely because the Giants are my family's ride-or-die football team! Up to that point, as a college student, I had little to read on the topic of celibacy besides Jesus' words on differentiated eunuchs (see Mt 19:12). Our Lord responded to my doubts on the matter with some specific lessons while I was reading the *Theology of the Body*.

One lesson came to me at my university gym. Every Thursday morning that semester, I would retreat to the room of punching bags after I worked out. Alone there,

---

1. For more information about how I discerned my vocation, see Opus Dei, "Angela Fortunato: public health administrator talks about finding her vocation," July 5, 2011, educational video, 9:46, https://opusdei.org/en/article/angela-fortunato-public-health-administrator-talks-about-finding-her-vocation/.

I would punch the bag with every fiber of my small physique, internally screaming at God (while exteriorly silent) for *giving me this crummy call to celibacy and not allowing me* to fall in love with one particular male classmate of mine. I felt that he was holding me back from what would most fulfill me.

Five months of Thursday tirades were answered one morning by a clarifying sense that if I would only stop kicking and screaming, I would realize that our Lord was not holding me back at all, but trying to embrace me. God always answers prayers, but sometimes he answers me in ways that are hard to ignore.

Toward the end of my college years, my mother passed away after fighting a chronic illness. My family had entrusted her petition for healing to St. Josemaría Escrivá, the founder of Opus Dei. God provided healing, but in a different way than we had asked. One way in particular was by giving me a spiritual boost. Heaven became real to me in a way that it hadn't previously: because my mother had now gone before God, certainly, but also because of my mother's relationship to her heavenly friends while she was on earth. Two interactions in particular with my mom stick in my memory from those years. In one, she invited me into the TV room to pray beside her while she continued speaking aloud to Jesus and his mother, as if they were physically present. In another, when I asked my mother if she was happy that one of my brothers and I had become numerary (celibate) members of Opus Dei,[2] she responded, "Well, I know you'll always be cared for." That response was quintessentially my Mom.

Taking that phrase from my mother, I composed a prayer of petition that expresses my desire to encourage and multiply new vocations, a prayer which I pray regularly and now offer to you:

> Lord, I give you permission to call anyone you want from among our families, our schools, our centers, and our apostolic work. And I, for my part, promise to take care of them. Amen.

2. Numeraries are celibate members of Opus Dei who "usually live in centers of Opus Dei, and are completely available to attend to the apostolic undertakings and the formation of the other faithful of the Prelature" of Opus Dei. See https://opusdei.org/en-us/article/members/.

## CHAPTER 1

# Being Like Christ: Celibacy in the Church

Why did Christ choose celibacy for himself? I do not pretend to know, but I do know that doing so was a countercultural move on his part. As we read in the Old Testament, marriage and progeny were the socially acceptable option for the Jewish people awaiting the Messiah. One theologian has called the shift from the fruitfulness of the flesh in the Old Testament to the fruitfulness of the spirit in the New Testament one of the key "turning points" in salvation history.[1]

1. Thomas McGovern, *Priestly Identity: A Study in the Theology of the Priesthood* (Dublin, Ireland: Four Courts Press, 2002), p. 102.

Every choice the Lord made here on earth has a deeper meaning, and his decision to live a celibate lifestyle was more than just countercultural: it established and directed the culture of Christianity at its foundation.

The virtue of Christian chastity becomes realized when we identify ourselves with the pure and chaste Christ and beg him to show us how to live like him. Both Christian marriage and celibacy, existing alongside one another within this new redemptive path set out by Christ, can seem so furiously difficult to live out successfully unless one receives special graces to do so.[2] Christ himself acknowledges this in Matthew 19, when his disciples lament the hardship of living his teachings about divorce and adultery: "The disciples said to him, 'If such is the case of a man with his wife, it is not expedient to marry.' But he said to them, 'Not all men can receive this precept, but only those to whom it is given'" (Mt 19:10–11).

---

2. See Romano Guardini, *The Lord* (Chicago: Henry Regnery Company, 1954), pp. 270–78.

In the verse that follows, we find Christ's famous words:

> Some are incapable of marriage because they were born so; some, because they were made so by others; some, because they have renounced marriage for the sake of the kingdom of heaven. Whoever can accept this ought to accept it.[3] (Mt 19:12)

Many scholars consider this a defense of Christ's own celibacy and that of many of his apostles.[4] When Christ answers questions about the kingdom of heaven, where "they neither marry nor are given in marriage, but are like angels in heaven" (Mk 12:25), he speaks directly of a spiritual fruitfulness that is eternal.

Of course, Christ is a Spouse and has a spouse. The Church is the bride of Christ, according to many Fathers of the Church. This spousal union continues to be extremely fruitful! "Christ's sacrifice is fruitful—that

3. NABRE translation.

4. See Michael E. Giesler, "Celibacy in the First Two Centuries," *Homiletic and Pastoral Review*, January 2009, Celibacy-in-the-first-Centuries.pdf, www.fathersofthechurch.com, p. 26.

is, paternal—because the salvific grace that he merited on the Cross is implanted in his spotless Bride, who raises up offspring in the order of grace."[5] Christ's fatherhood is a paramount attribute for those priests and other celibate men for whom paternity is part of their vocational fulfillment. And, since the Church raises those offspring, who are "born from his side on the Cross,"[6] women can also identify with this attribute of Christ in his life-bearing self-sacrifice.

Indeed, the starting point in the history of celibacy in the Church begins with Christ himself. And, of course, we encounter the Holy Family, surrounding each other with love. The Catholic Church teaches the perpetual virginity of Mary before, during, and after the birth of Jesus. She is often depicted in artwork as present in a maternal role at the birth of the Church at Pentecost. Joseph, too, had a celibate calling for the sake of the higher mission of caring for the Messiah.

---

5. Carter Griffin, *Why Celibacy: Reclaiming the Fatherhood of the Priest* (Steubenville, Ohio: Emmaus Road Publishing, 2019), p. 7.

6. Griffin, p. 7.

In the Holy Family, we see the unity between marriage and celibacy. They also visualize for us the priority of family life, made strong through daily acts of mutual self-giving, constant communication, and lots of caring, joy, and laughter. In his article "Celibacy in the First Centuries," Fr. Michael Giesler concludes, "It is clear then that the origin of virginity or celibacy is intrinsically connected with love for God, and as a result of that love, with evangelization."[7]

Fr. Giesler continues, "without question the power and appeal of celibacy in the first two centuries came above all from the direct example of Jesus Christ, his mother and the apostles, and from the dedicated lives of both male and female Christians."[8] For example, the apostolic era written about in the New Testament mentions several women among the men who directly followed Jesus and who were among the first ones to spread the Good News after his Death, Resurrection, and Ascension—Lydia, Dorcas, Rhoda, and Mary Magdalene, to name a few.

---

7. Giesler, p. 30.

8. Giesler, p. 30.

In his first letter to the Corinthians, St. Paul directly addresses his state of celibacy, saying, "I wish that all were as I myself am. But each has his own special gift from God, one of one kind and one of another" (1 Cor 7:7). He then gives advice to the unmarried and to widows: ". . . it is well for them to remain single as I do" (1 Cor 7:8). "In immediate post-apostolic times we have clear testimony that men and women throughout the Roman Empire had received the charism of celibacy and lived it fervently," says Giesler.[9] We do not have complete records of many of these devout celibate followers, but we can find references to their existence. One written document that has survived from the first century of the Church (AD 95) is the letter of Pope Clement (Clement of Rome) to the Corinthians. Pope Clement addresses those living celibacy with this advice: "Let him who is continent not boast of it—knowing that it is another that giveth him the power of continence."[10]

---

9. Giesler, p. 28.

10. Clement of Rome, "Letter to Corinthians" from *Ancient Christian Writers*, eds. J. Quasten and Joseph Plumpe (Westminster, MD: The Newman Bookshop, 1946), p. 32.

Priestly celibacy was well-established by the 4th century Councils[11] and has repeatedly been supported by subsequent councils and synods. The first centuries after Christ were the beginnings of the Christian celibate hermit life; then emerged the religious orders around the 5th century, with a myriad of religious orders for women by the middle ages. In most societies throughout human history, a woman's property rights were tied up with her father's or her husband's. Unless independently wealthy as their father's heir or belonging to a religious order, most women in history were expected to marry. Since the foundation of religious orders, then, the Church has continued to be the context in which many great women have found their place to flourish in life and in society, and in many cases, to successfully lead others.

Let's consider St. Macrina the Younger, an early Christian consecrated virgin known for her purity, sanctity, and asceticism; or St. Scholastica, an Italian hermit and foundress of the Benedictine nuns.

11. Griffin, p. 56.

St. Hildegard of Bingen, a Benedictine abbess, left an indelible imprint on Christianity as a composer of sacred music, philosopher, medical practitioner, and mystic. St. Catherine of Siena never married, nor did she take the veil: instead, her celibate life was one of piety and mysticism, and also of papal and secular politics, leading to her eventually being declared a Doctor of the Church. St. Teresa of Avila, the first woman declared Doctor of the Church, was author of the famous *The Interior Castle* and reformed the flailing religious lifestyle of the times. Thérèse of Lisieux—yet another Doctor of the Church!—in her twenty-four short years of life, revitalized Christian piety with her Little Way. Edith Stein, born into an observant Jewish family, was a brilliant philosopher who found Christianity and celibacy later in life, taking Discalced Carmelite vows and becoming a martyr during World War II. Her contemporary, St. Faustina Kowalska, a mystic known as the Apostle of Divine Mercy, lived her celibacy as a nun and left a legacy of pure love and devotion to Christ through her *Diary*.

These women are the tip of the iceberg of celibate women who found their path to holiness through dedicated celibacy with and for the Church.

My story and ponderings in these pages share the experience of celibacy lived out in the 20th and 21st centuries, since that is when God brought about the foundation of Opus Dei, a personal prelature of the Church, through St. Josemaría Escrivá. My written reflections pertain to apostolic celibacy as it is lived out as a member of Opus Dei.

You may wonder why I gloss over centuries of vocations to consecrated virginity, of women who have found their identity as a bride of Christ. Certainly, I have high regard for the countless dedicated and generous women who discover their Christian identity and mission in religious life! Over the years, I have had the delight of helping two young women discern and discover God-given paths in religious life. Two is exactly double the number of nuns that I met growing up! My great aunt Sr. Laetizia was a Mother Cabrini nun in Australia and visited us in New Jersey. I don't recall ever seeing another nun before attending large Papal audiences. In other words, the knowledge I share with you in this book flows from what I know from experience: my life and the lives of others, in and of the Church, through lay (not religious) Christian celibacy.

In his book on the Second Vatican Council,[12] George Weigel says that the legacy of that Council is the centrality of the person of Jesus Christ. Let this little book be a drop in the bucket to that great end, then, of keeping Jesus Christ at the center of celibacy. Christ's Holy Family is my reference point. Because Christ is alive, he is my contemporary model for living celibacy in a fulfilling and fruitful way.

---

12. George Weigel, *To Sanctify the World: The Vital Legacy of Vatican II* (New York: Basic Books, 2022).

## CHAPTER 2

# Being Offered a Hundredfold

Have you ever asked Jesus about his "hundredfold" promise? He promises, "And everyone who has left houses or brothers or sisters or father or mother or wife or children or fields for my sake will receive a hundred times as much and will inherit eternal life" (Mt 19:29). Propelled by self-interest, I found myself asking Jesus repeatedly about what he meant by an earthly payoff in addition to a heavenly one. Once, I heard an answer to my conundrum from an unlikely place: my own mouth! When discussing with a married couple their daughter's discernment of a vocation to apostolic celibacy, I asked them each to consider what God provides to them that a spouse cannot, then to take that difference and multiply it by one hundred in both quality and quantity in order to begin to see what God offers me in celibacy. While speaking to them about the beauty of apostolic celibacy, God spoke to my own heart.

One could focus on how, for example, God created me, sustains me, and knows me better than any husband ever could. Jesus, who multiplied the loaves and fishes to give sustenance to the crowds in the Gospels, is the Great Multiplier in my own life on earth. I don't bring any more to the equation than everything I am and everything I have, just like the boy in the crowd who brought five loaves and two fish that day (see Jn 6:9). It is God who works in powers of ten and in exponentials when apostolic celibacy is involved. Of course, every Christian is called to give himself or herself wholeheartedly to God, but it is God who brings the "greater" to the relationship when he offers that person the gift of celibacy in the Church.

I'd like to highlight three areas in which a person who accepts the Lord's gift of apostolic celibacy receives a hundredfold of divine gifts: their interior life, apostolic life, and social life.

## INTERIOR LIFE

For every baptized Christian, the interior life, otherwise known as the prayer life, develops around the person of Jesus Christ. He is the fundamental answer to questions of identity and mission such as: "Who am I?" and "For whom am I?" Just as some married persons have deeper interior lives than others, some celibate apostles have deeper interior lives than others. When I say that a person living apostolic celibacy receives a hundredfold of divine gifts in their interior life, I'm not comparing depth and holiness between different people in different vocations—that would be theologically problematic. The key point is that God brings the multiplying factor to the equation, resulting in a profoundly fulfilling answer to those dilemmas of identity and mission that every person must answer. When living solely for God, God as the answer is deeply satisfying. In God's mysterious manner, the relationship between God and the soul who responds affirmatively to his gratuitous gift of apostolic celibacy is more intimate than it would be between God and that soul had he or she never responded to that gift. I will try to clarify this point with a metaphor.

As a teenager, my interior life benefited from many metaphors and images based on what I was reading from St. Josemaría. I used my imagination in this way to purify my interior senses that had too easily fallen into the bad habit of daydreaming. Through my imagination, I came to understand the freedom of responding to a call through the metaphor of a softball mitt. God stands ready to pitch me a softball, which in this case symbolizes the gift of celibacy. And he desperately wants me to catch it. He looks to see if I have my mitt on and if it is held in a position that shows I am ready to catch what he is about to throw. He will not throw the ball if he doesn't find me ready, willingly and freely holding up my mitt.

The best advice I can give to young people considering their vocation, then, is to pray explicitly to God in direct words that amount to something like this:

"Go ahead, God! Tell me or show me your will, and I will respond with a resounding *Yes*, because I trust that your will is good and is meant for my greatest happiness!" I advise these young people to show their openness and trust in God by going to him in the sacraments and committing to a regular and sincere prayer life. Participating in what you already know is God's will for you by showing him that you're already saying yes to whatever his will is for you—even though you don't know all of what it means—is like putting up your mitt for the catch. God doesn't pitch apostolic celibacy to every unmarried person, but I get the acute sense in prayer that he would offer a hundredfold in this life to many more young people if only more of them would simply hold up their mitts.

Two more images invaded my mental prayer, almost like recurrent dreams, when I considered these unmerited graces that I had received. In one image, I was hurriedly working my way through a dense forest with a machete in my hand. Intuitively, I understood that building habits of prayer was hard work, and spiritual callouses marked my hands as I would swing my arm to push forward inch by inch. I made little headway and felt discouraged as I saw how many virtues I lacked and how badly I followed through with my resolutions. Suddenly, my perspective changed when I responded affirmatively to God asking me to give my whole life to him. The prayerful image shifted to a bird's-eye view, and the dense wood fell away. Tight little paths opened up ahead of me; I could then run at full speed. My prayer life became easier, clearer, and more effective because of something that God did: he changed my perspective after I gave him permission.

## APOSTOLIC LIFE

The third image I experienced within my prayer presented graces as raindrops from the skies. Accepting God's offer of the gift of celibacy was like allowing a powerful flood of rain to descend and saturate the dry earth. If the graces given into a life of apostolic celibacy are multiplied a hundredfold like a shower pouring down upon earth, there would simply be too many for one person to absorb! These graces, brought down through apostolic celibacy, are also meant for others who benefit from a nourished earth. In sharing this analogy, though, I also must affirm that the primary person God brings closest to himself through apostolic celibacy is always the one called.

I would primarily define *apostolate* as the sharing of the life and love of Jesus Christ with those around you. Inasmuch as I abandon myself into God's hands, the Holy Spirit will reach out to whomever he wants, usually without any planning on my part. Being an apostle is, then, a natural overflow of one's interior life. I learned from Pope John Paul II to include in my morning offering an open permission to the Holy Spirit to reach whomever he wants in my life that day. I've witnessed great spiritual blessings in people's lives as a result.

## SOCIAL LIFE

I want to emphasize a few dimensions of the widespread social life that accompanies apostolic celibacy. By social life, I mean one's life in society and in the nucleus of society that is the family. Those who welcome the flood of graces that accompany the gift of apostolic celibacy consequently become better friends insofar as they are united to Christ as their best friend. The list of my faults and weaknesses as a friend would be much longer and grimmer without that closest friendship with Christ in my life. A similar thing could be said about my life as a student and classmate, and as a worker and colleague. As far as Christ is my first love and my best friend, his love enlarges my heart and fills my heart with his divine love.

In *The Way of the Cross*, St. Josemaría writes that "the human heart is endowed with an enormous coefficient of expansion. When it loves, it opens out in a crescendo of affection that overcomes all barriers."[1] When praying as a teenager, I often imagined this expansion like a balloon that God pumped up inside my heart, allowing room for every other worthy love to fit inside. Loves incompatible with divine love would be burned

---

1. Josemaría Escrivá, *The Way of the Cross* (New York: Scepter, 2002), p.55.

up by his love. But every other love would fit, excluding no one I held in my heart from experiencing his love for them. I used to pray and offer my permission to the Holy Spirit to pump away in my heart and purify as needed. Although my day-to-day relationships were made up of more failures than successes, these images facilitated my conversation with the Lord in a way that helped me persevere in love and increase my requests for his divine assistance.

CHAPTER 3

# Being in the Midst of the World

There are quite obviously many differences between apostolic celibacy and marriage. But when considered more carefully, it becomes clear that apostolic celibacy and Christian marriage function as close collaborators on the same team, almost as two sides of the same coin. To live my vocation happily, I have had to become very knowledgeable about the vocation of Christian marriage. One motive for writing this book is to help more married people to appreciate celibacy to the extent that they would be overjoyed to have a family member or dear friend answer this wondrous call from God.

In my twenties, I started mentoring married women, and it repeatedly struck me how similar my celibate life was to theirs. Commitment to a Christian life in the midst of the world, particularly to those women living the tenets of Opus Dei, meant that we had a great deal in common. During those years, I wrote my own "Litany of Humility" and a "Litany of Working Accompanied by Jesus" to pray for myself and for other women who had struggles similar to mine. These litanies are a sort of twenty-first-century version of the classic prayer written by Cardinal Merry del Val. Here is a sampling:

From the idea that I know best, **deliver me, Jesus.**
From the idea that I can do it better or more quickly, **deliver me, Jesus.**
From passing judgments or comparisons, **deliver me, Jesus.**
From making exaggerations, excuses, or embellishments, **deliver me, Jesus.**
From voicing "the scoop," **deliver me, Jesus.**

Help me to listen to others till the end,
**thus, fill my heart with your Love.**

Help me to thank others and you!, **thus, fill my heart with your Love.**
Help me to take corrections well and to learn, **thus, fill my heart with your Love.**
Help me to ask for help, **thus, fill my heart with your Love.**
Help me to act my age always, **thus, fill my heart with your Love.**

That I be as productive as God wants today, **thus may I sense you there with me, Jesus.**
That I be able to be interrupted today, **thus may I sense you there with me, Jesus.**
That my teams enjoy synergy, **thus may I sense you there with me, Jesus.**
That I work ethically well and set a good example, **thus may I sense you there with me, Jesus.**
For apostolic fruit from all we do, **thus may I sense you there with me, Jesus.**
That every experience of the Cross while working brings me closer to your Sacred Heart, **thus may I sense you there with me, Jesus.**

When listening to other women talk about their struggles, I noticed that the players and places differed, certainly, but the content of the day-to-day struggles, victories, and defeats was familiar. Working and living in a family, caring for the young and old, worrying about finances and maintenance repairs—these make up a daily panorama where God can be found and forgotten and then found again.

I was raised watching Disney princess movies, which formed a naive idea of what married life encompassed. So, I was surprised to see so little difference between life with and without a so-called Prince Charming. Comparatively, the vast difference between life with and without God became crystal clear, especially during those years I spent in graduate school and in university hospitals, where the hookup culture dominated. I would regularly give a talk to young women on retreats about the virtue of holy purity, and I began refining my talking points to align Christian marriage and apostolic celibacy as a singular countercultural alternative to the hookup culture. Married women supported me in my vocation, and I supported them in theirs; we were teammates in cultivating a healthy environment in which to raise their families, and we worked together to raise the "spiritual temperature" of our city's university and hospital campuses.

One of the best parts of following a collegiate calendar for over a decade was to have summers free to help run girls' camps. At every camp session, I tried to make it out to the swimming pool at least once while the girls swam. I found these moments great opportunities to engage them in conversation. One pool chat with an elementary-school-age camper sticks in my memory. The camper had asked me about my life as a numerary and was trying to make sense of my vocation by comparing me to a nun. We tallied up the similarities of my life to a nun's with only three fingers: I was Catholic, a woman, and I had given my life to God by not getting married.

But then we continued, at my suggestion, to tally up what made me like her mother. I don't live in a religious community, and an Opus Dei center is a true Christian home. I had the same "plan of life" (habits to help you grow closer to God)[1] as her mom, who happened to be a supernumerary[2] member of Opus Dei. The list of similarities went on and on. Her mom and I participated in many of the same activities, from daily prayers and frequent sacraments, to balancing full-time work outside the home with responsibilities for home life, to caring for young people and old people in our families, with my "family" including individuals participating in Opus Dei formational activities. Rounding out our list were some coincidental similarities, as well: her mom and I lived in the same city, were about the same age, and had similar work schedules. The differences in our lives were so few, which became a sort of epiphany in my own comprehension of God's harmonious plan for the solidarity of both marriage and

---

1. See Opus Dei, ""Plan of Life: Habits to Help You Grow Closer to God," https://opusdei.org/en-us/article/plan-of-life-habits-to-help-you-grow-closer-to-god/.

2. A lay faithful who is generally a married man or woman who participates in the apostolates of Opus Dei and "for whom the sanctification of their family duties is the most important part of their Christian life." Opus Dei, "Christians in the Middle of the World," https://opusdei.org/en-us/article/members/.

celibacy, working side-by-side in the world with the common goal of bringing about his kingdom through our ordinary lives. We concluded that my life was a lot more like her mom's than a religious sister's but recognized that nuns also shared the deep bond of Catholicism and womanhood.

If I were to view celibacy and marriage as opposites, I would imagine my life bereft of a "Prince Charming," and epic love songs like Aerosmith's "I Don't Want to Miss a Thing" would be absolute torture for me to listen to. Instead, I sing along karaoke-style and at the top of my lungs, because I am on the same team as Christian marriage. In an age of great confusion about marriage, I, faithfully living apostolic celibacy, am a strong defender and cheerleader for marriage. When explaining this in abbreviated terms, I usually say that I gave up my own marriage so that I could help encourage and support the sacrament of marriage through many, many individual marriages.

That particular day at the pool, I did not explain to the young camper that her mom would not have had the opportunity to become a supernumerary member of Opus Dei unless, first, some men and women had been willing to answer the call to the celibate numerary vocation. The numeraries and associates[3] provide continuity in the institution throughout space and time. St. Josemaría put it this way: "In order that many may employ the 'I,' 'you,' and 'he' of personal apostolate in all their fullness, a group of dedicated, competent, and apostolic men and women have to employ the anonymous 'we.'"[4] It is not about relative holiness or relative value; it is a matter of relative availability to foster the continued existence of the institution of Opus Dei.

When I decided to respond to God's invitation to celibacy, I was neither thinking of preserving the

---

3. "Some faithful of the Prelature are men and women who commit themselves to celibacy, for apostolic reasons. Associates live with their families, or wherever is convenient for professional reasons," in contrast to numeraries who "usually live in centers of Opus Dei, and are completely available to attend to the apostolic undertakings and the formation of the other faithful of the Prelature." Opus Dei, "Christians in the Middle of the World," https://opusdei.org/en-us/article/members/.

4. Josemaría Escrivá, "Instruction on the Work of Saint Gabriel," in the draft from May 1935 and in the finished text from September 14, 1950, no. 100.

institution of marriage nor the institution of Opus Dei. As I said in an interview for the Opus Dei website, I can think of no better reason for celibacy than the personal call of God.[5] It was our Lord's face and his tone of voice that caught my attention, spoke to my heart, and still sustain me as I dedicate my life to the Christian formation of others. When I ponder just how much God is working with and through celibacy in the midst of the world, I am revived, and I petition God for the continued needs of his Church.

---

5. Opus Dei, "Members of Opus Dei," February 23, 2016, educational video, 4:04, https://opusdei.org/en-us/article/members-of-opus-dei/.

CHAPTER 4

# Being Comfortable with Insecurity and Uncertainty

In a book of interviews titled *Conversations*, St. Josemaría says, "Only among those who understand and value in all its depth . . . human love can there arise another ineffable insight of which Jesus speaks [see Mt 19:11–12]: an insight which is a pure gift of God, moving a person to dedicate body and soul to the Lord, to offer him an undivided heart, without the mediation of earthly love."[1] As a Christian wife, a woman finds herself by giving herself wholeheartedly to God,

1. Josemaría Escrivá, *Conversations with Saint Josemaría Escrivá* (New York: Scepter, 2007), no. 122.

mediated through the gift of herself to her husband. There is, then, a simplicity in the lack of mediation for the person called to celibacy.

Pope Benedict XVI wrote about celibacy using biblical exegesis when he referred to the Jewish people in the Jubilee Years and to the priestly house of Levi, both of whom put their trust wholeheartedly in God. He explained that those who respond to God's invitation to celibacy live without the security that comes from building one's own home, having one's own children and ancestral line, and accumulating one's own assets (see Mt 19:29). This message of abandonment to divine providence is really for every Christian follower. The celibate person provides a helpful example to everyone of the value of divine security in our consumerist society that is constantly shouting contrary messages. The celibate person stands opposite the man described by Jesus in Luke 12:16–20, who takes security in his own harvest and builds bigger and bigger barns for a future that would never come to him.

Putting one's whole life and self into God's hands at the start of one's life story in celibacy involves not knowing what the future chapters will hold. More importantly, it involves trusting that those chapters will be better written with God as the author. It involves trust in God alone. Although it doesn't rid life of worry, it provides the antidote to such worry. Apostolic celibacy in the midst of the world is a preemptive strike on the false securities of this life and a witness to the value of placing our trust in God repeatedly. Responding affirmatively to God's gift of celibacy provides a certain immunity from being overly concerned about what others think about us. Trusting in God alone helps us live before his eyes alone.

*Availability* is a term that can help us understand the unity of the vocation to Opus Dei even as we distinguish the modalities, or ways of being a member. Pope Benedict XVI warned against an overly pragmatic definition of availability when he said, "The reference to greater availability is not enough: such a greater availability of time could easily become also a form of egoism that saves a person from the sacrifices and efforts demanded by the reciprocal acceptance and forbearance in matrimony; thus, it could lead to a spiritual impoverishment or to hardening of the heart."[2]

Availability has multiple positive meanings, and I will focus here on these three: availability to move physically, availability of heart, and availability of mind.

## AVAILABILITY TO MOVE PHYSICALLY

As I said previously, numeraries and associates, the celibate members, provide the continuity of Opus Dei through both time and space. By this I mean that each new generation of numeraries and associates, by sustaining the other members, ensures that Opus Dei will continue to exist through at least that generation in a given geographic area. Numeraries may move, sometimes many times in their lifetime, in order to better serve the various formational needs of Opus Dei across different geographic areas.

This is slightly different from the situation of a wife who moves homes to meet the needs of her immediate family or even her extended family. A wife moves her

2. Benedict XVI, Address to the Roman Curia, December 22, 2006.

household with all the factors of her security—her husband, her children, her family heirlooms, her household items, her bank account—and places her future life in that new place into God's hands. This move demands quite an adventurous spirit from a wife, who must continue to support her husband and family through these changing circumstances.

In contrast, the same circumstances that make a numerary or associate more available can also make her less secure. The first numeraries came to the United States from Spain with one small suitcase, a few dollars, and an image of the Blessed Mother, their gift from St. Josemaría. (I would gladly trade my multiple modern suitcases and FedEx boxes for a chance to meet the founder of Opus Dei and to receive his blessing!) It must have been both thrilling and a little scary to come to a new country with so little. Modern living comes with a lot of stuff, and it takes hard work and a willingness of heart and mind to give away generously and to pack lightly. Moving with very few factors of security helps me focus on the one thing I know I take with me, which is Our Lord himself.

## AVAILABILITY OF HEART

Availability of heart is the act of allowing Christ to fill one's heart with his love and his life, which can then overflow into the people around us. Availability should certainly be lived fully by all Christians! This availability of heart is made easier by the avoidance of attachment to the *things* of this life in order to be more attached to *God* and available to the individuals he places in our lives.

For people who live in the midst of the material world, it can be easy to get attached to things. This means that the Christian virtues of poverty and detachment must be fought for. St. Josemaría frequently gave specific pieces of practical advice on living these virtues: "Don't hold on to anything as if it were your own . . . Have nothing superfluous . . . Don't complain when you lack something necessary . . . When the choice is up to you, take the poorest thing, whatever is least desirable . . . Don't mistreat the objects you use . . . Make good use of time."[3]

3. Cesare Cavalleri, *40 Years With a Saint: Blessed Alvaro del Portillo on Saint Josemaría Escrivá* (New York: Scepter Publishers, 2016), p. 148.

Along with the gift of celibacy comes the grace to live poverty and detachment according to St. Josemaría's challenging words. Of course, it is an uphill battle in a consumerist, individualistic society. It is not that the celibate person finds this poverty and detachment easy, but there is a certain ease that comes from practicing a good habit. She is helped a great deal by divine assistance and is guided by the practical advice of St. Josemaría. Answering the call to a celibate vocation is an act of detachment in itself, and within this vocation a celibate person grows accustomed to a joyful living of uncertainty and insecurity, naturally leading to a greater ease of detachment. A celibate person, then, can be a visible witness to others, showing them that detachment from things is possible and that we can live in the midst of the world without allowing worldly cares to dominate our feelings and attitudes.

I think here of what St. Josemaría wrote in *The Way* about how much worse the daily communicant would be without having received Communion, even though he or she sees so little progress. "Receiving Communion every day for so many years! Anybody else would be a saint by now—you told me—and I . . . I'm always the same! Son, I replied, keep up your daily Communion, and think: What would I be if I hadn't received?"[4] I would say that this lesson applies very well to poverty and detachment. We would all be much more attached to things without having received so many graces to help us make specific acts of detachment.

There's a word that helps explain this concept of having and using things while being detached from them: *secularity*. Secularity means caring deeply about what is happening in society as just one more member of that society. Secularity and detachment are compatible. Indeed, the world needs the witness of both qualities harmoniously working together. It is reasonable and virtuous to be countercultural when the culture is materialistic. However, we become no less "secular" just because we are noticeably detached from earthly goods.

Men and women who observe apostolic celibacy have the advantage of a different kind of security—

4. Josemaría Escrivá, *The Way* (New York: Scepter Publishers, 2010), no. 534.

divine security. The idea of availability of heart is also a particular call to parents of numeraries. As I had previously shared, my mother told me that she knew my numerary brother and I would always be well cared for. She mentioned this to me, though, with a bit of sadness, knowing that we would not usually make it home for family holidays and that we would not give her any grandchildren. With great availability of heart, she overcame that sadness. She became proud of us, and she allowed her heart to expand with joy in our vocations.

Most parents, in fact, have trouble accepting when a child of theirs embraces a life of apostolic celibacy. God's gift of this particular vocation to a person includes a sense of appreciation, acceptance, and comfort with insecurity as well as an immunity to caring about what others think of them. My wish is that their parents also receive such comfort and immunity! While a child's celibate vocation demands a heroic detachment on behalf of the parents, I ask them to find some comfort where my mother found it: in the certainty that their child will be well cared for.

In God's abundant mercy, there is much grace for parents in the gift of giving their child to the Lord, more than knowing their child will rest in good hands. They can also take heart knowing that they will be the recipients of the watershed of graces overflowing in the lives of their children willing to answer God's call. These special graces include witnessing their child live a rich and happy life, filled with a loving community, generous self-giving, meaningful work, and personal fulfillment. All parents deeply want their children to be good people with happy lives. Parents of people called to celibacy see this wish fulfilled.

Christ, in his divinity and humanity, is the source of the self-giving love in both marriage and celibacy. If Christ is the source of true love and fulfillment, one should trust that giving oneself totally to him is never a liability but always an indescribable blessing!

## AVAILABILITY OF MIND

Availability of mind, another application of this secular spirit, is an openness to be knowledgeable of the goings-on in the world as a way to engage others and help bring them closer to God. The secular spirit of Opus Dei is contrary to any "bubble" mentality that seeks to hide from the ugly features of reality. We resist any spirit that would have us retreat to the catacombs. The very root of the word *apostle* means "one who is sent"—we are sent out to the world, and so we must know the world.

All of Christ's disciples, married and celibate, must obtain a prodigious availability of mind. I am edified by the many Christian men and women who work hard to become learned and well-read, positively influencing society on an intellectual level. A person living apostolic celibacy possesses the advantage of an ease to commit time and energy to study, without the responsibilities that come with a spouse and children. Thus, there is a greater sense of responsibility to cultivate this availability of mind, and it is quite a shame when I do not study as well and as much as I should!

CHAPTER 5

# Being at the Foot of the Cross

Suffering is invariably a part of everyone's earthly life. One secret of happiness for the Christian is to reframe each occasion of suffering as an opportunity to embrace our Lord himself, and thus to express one's love for God's will in deeds. Sometimes it has taken me months to discover the joy of a particular experience with the cross, but the discovery of joy has always coincided with the discovery of precisely how Christ was accompanying me in my suffering.

I mentioned already that Pope St. John Paul II has been a prominent figure in my life. I'd like to share how I once met him one-on-one. In 2002, I traveled to Rome for a conference celebrating the one-hundredth anniversary of the birth of St. Josemaría. *I* traveled to Rome, but *my luggage* did not. During my first night in the hotel, I prayed as if making a deal: "OK, God, you are clearly in charge. If I were in charge, I would have my luggage. Since I don't have my luggage, you are in charge. Surprise me!"

Always faithful, the Lord surprised me by taking charge in all sorts of ways! I did not see any of the sights I had hoped to see; instead, I conversed with inspiring people from all over the world. I brought home no fine Italian leather goods, as I had planned; instead, I brought home an amazing memory of speaking directly with Bishop Javier Echevarría, who was the prelate of Opus Dei at that time.

Happy to have heard his commentary on the great work being done in my country, I headed back to my hotel room—and soon found myself in an encompassing physical misery. I bled from every orifice of my body except my eyes and ears, and I endured the waves of pain only by imitating what little I knew about how a woman is supposed to breathe while delivering a baby. After several hours of agony, every ounce of food having been violently ejected from my body, the pain subsided and I army-crawled to my bed, my legs unable to bear my body weight. I begged God for help, but mostly for mercy, wanting desperately to sleep, but unsure when and if I would wake again. After falling asleep, I did wake up, though I did not dare eat for a while. I surprisingly felt well enough to walk to a nearby Mass and then into the scheduled audience with the pope in the Paul VI Audience Hall. I flopped into a seat in the back row with minutes to spare; soon, I was ushered forward, having been picked out of the crowd to take a seat inside the papal stage area. Looking back, I believe that I would not have been chosen had I arrived as planned and been seated with my friends.

I knelt down in front of the saintly pope, allowed him to bless me, and said, "In Pittsburgh, in the USA, we are good watchmen of the *Tertio Millenio*." Unprepared for this visit, I was wearing the same outfit that I had worn on the plane and on most days of the trip. Standing by the Holy Father, Bishop Echevarría had in his hands a list of those who had been pre-selected to meet the Holy Father. I was invariably not on the list, but to my surprise, he remembered me from the night before and proceeded to tell the pope who I was. God certainly took charge on that day!

Pope John Paul II was at an advanced stage of his life in which he saved his words, but his gaze at me spoke volumes. If you also had the good fortune to meet him, you understand when I say that his glance was loving, deep, and sincere, a pure *agape* love, surpassing a love brought about by romance. From his *Theology of the Body*, I had learned about the theory of the gift of celibacy. From his look at me, I learned the practicality of a life given over to others in a universal manner, *precisely because it is a life given over to God.* It is an all-encompassing self-giving because it is not exclusive to one spouse; universal, and yet individual. I can sincerely say that Pope John Paul II loved me as an individual in that moment. In fact, it felt as if there were no one else in that auditorium!

That glance modeled for me how I should live my own celibacy, open to every person yet simultaneously personal. While in prayer, I have since reminded Pope

John Paul II, now in his heavenly abode, about how much he prayed for me and loved me that day. For decades, I petitioned him to teach me how to prioritize people before tasks. I have more recently started petitioning him to teach me to see people with the eyes of Christ, just as he did. Pope John Paul II surely knew how to share the life and love of Jesus Christ with those around him, and sometimes he did so without uttering even one word.

That is my story about meeting a pope. It is also my story about getting diagnosed with celiac disease. I did not ask St. Josemaría to cure me for his one-hundredth birthday, but that diagnosis was certainly his birthday present to me since it set me on a clear path toward better health. He also gave me what I had asked him for, which was the arrival of my luggage immediately before my return trip. I never opened the bag until I was safely back in the United States.

Being humiliated and built back up again by God through a chronic illness is its own long story. But suffice it to say that I received both the medical care and the spiritual help that I needed in order to fully embrace this part of my path toward God. My list of daily sacrifices now includes those things I should do to stay healthy, which for me is a pretty short list that focuses on not eating gluten. I also learned other lessons: about my own physical and psychological limitations, about depending more on God in practical ways, and about asking others for help.

My medical history now includes a five-year fight with Lyme disease and a five-month stint of scabies, both ending in complete cures and both involving neurological symptoms. God alone knows every detail of this journey, and indeed, has allowed it for my greater good.

Although much of the suffering I share here has been physical, I do want to acknowledge that psychological suffering is much harder at the spiritual level. The reason for this is that psychological suffering inevitably involves the other hardest type of suffering: interpersonal suffering. I have lived with a few saints who are surely now in heaven and who endured serious psychological difficulties. In hindsight, I see that their hardships were a significant part of their path to God. I was part of the interpersonal component of their lives and their suffering, so their challenges were also a part of my own path to God, when I chose to embrace them as such.

The gaze of Christ is merciful, loving, and universal. I continue to ask Pope St. John Paul II to teach me how to unexclusively and unreservedly offer that loving gaze to others, especially to those suffering in any way. Among the graces open to me with my calling to apostolic celibacy are those that facilitate my sharing of the life and love of Christ with anyone around me. Being at the foot of the Cross of Christ means finding him there. Staying at the foot of the Cross of Christ means finding him in others who are there as well.

CHAPTER 6

# Being a "Beloved Disciple"

In his Gospel, St. John calls himself "the one whom Jesus loved." Tradition tells us that he was the youngest of the twelve and one who lived a vocation to celibacy for the sake of the Church. As a celibate person, he was available to care for Jesus' mother. Although perhaps not the only celibate apostle, we know he was special, even among the select. Yet, in the Gospels, we find no obvious reason to think that John had any outstanding natural qualities. One thing he did possess was youth: he was young enough to put his entire adulthood into Jesus' hands, so that Jesus could determine what that adulthood would consist of, and where it would be lived, and for whom.[1]

On the night Jesus was betrayed, John rested his head on our Lord's chest, and so he felt the change in heartbeat as Jesus predicted the betrayal. When the Lord's foreboding proved true, all the disciples abandoned him, except John. St. Josemaría noted that "at the moment of truth, they all fled, except for John who truly loved with deeds. Only the adolescent, youngest of the apostles, can be found next to the cross."[2]

St. John Henry Newman observed that Jesus favored John with affection and then entrusted his own mother to John's care. For these reasons, John could become a "memorial and pattern (as far as man can be) of love, deep, contemplative, fervent, unruffled, unbounded."[3]

---

1. In this chapter I will follow St. John as he is portrayed in the Italian book *Come Gesù*, by Fr. Mauro Leonardi (Milan: Ares, 2011). The author follows the youngest apostle through the last episodes of Jesus' life—the Last Supper through the Crucifixion. I borrow many of Fr. Leonardi's ideas, as his book has not yet been translated into English.

2. Josemaría Escrivá, *Christ Is Passing By: Homilies by Josemaría Escrivá* (New York: Scepter, 1982), no. 2.

3. John Henry Newman, *Parochial and Plain Sermons*, vol. 2 (London: Rivingtons, 1869), sermon 5: "Love of Relations and Friends," p. 56.

John certainly found strength in the example of Mary, and so he was able to be present at the foot of the Cross. He was strengthened by the Blessed Mother precisely to give more consolation to Jesus and to provide more support to his Church as he suffered. All of this is linked to John's particular apostolic celibacy.

Whenever I face suffering—physical, psychological, spiritual, or interpersonal—I look to the cause and ask myself whether Christ is offended by this same thing, because holding on to a sorrow that God does not share could actually offend him. If he is offended, then I seek first and foremost to offer consolation to our Lord. But if Christ is not offended by the thing that causes me suffering or worry, then I ask God's help to simply let it go.

In this way, it is my desire to be nailed to the Cross, so that I cannot go far from where Christ is, where I can console him. The only real suffering in the end is to miss out on Christ in the hide-and-seek he plays with us, in our suffering. To kiss only the wood of the Cross and not to kiss the wounds of Christ would lead to my misery. His presence brings the light and the lightness to my journey with the Cross.

St. John could love with the heart of Christ because his own heart synced up with the heartbeat of Our Lord at the Last Supper. Have you ever allowed the Holy Spirit to get your heart in sync with our Lord's heart? Maybe you don't readily think of your Eucharistic Communions and times before the tabernacle in those terms, but that is what happens there if you let it.

Consider a principle from the physics of waves: the frequency of a wave is the same as the frequency of the source of energy that produces that wave. When I kneel before the tabernacle, I often combine this physics lesson with the scene of St. John resting his head on Christ's chest. I beg Christ to get my heart in sync with his, so as to love anyone and everyone I meet, to love them with my heart—but with my heart as it is transformed by the love of Christ. Otherwise, I cannot share his love and his life with others, which is how I define my apostolic mission.[4] This synchronization is available to every Christian, and in particular every Christian who lives a Eucharistic life.

4. See Escrivá, *The Way*, no. 884.

So what difference does the gift of apostolic celibacy make here? St. John the Apostle is a saint for the entire Church, but it is significant that he is specifically a patron of love. His was a celibate, *agape* love, a magnetically Christological love that is a paragon for those young people to whom God offers the gift of celibacy. St. Josemaría expresses his confidence in the intercession of St. John when he says:

> How frankly you laughed when I advised you to put your youthful years under the protection of Saint Raphael, "so that he'll lead you, as he did young Tobias, to a holy marriage, with a girl who is good and pretty—and rich," I added jokingly. And then how thoughtful you became, when I went on to advise you to put yourself also under the patronage of that youthful Apostle John, in case God were to ask more of you.[5]

The total trust that celibate persons place in God makes it easier for them not to trust the fickle nature of their own hearts and their own minds. I need that

5. Escrivá, *The Way*, no. 360.

synchronizing communion with Christ because I trust his heart, not my own, to love people the way that they deserve to be loved.

After my years in academia and university hospitals, I decided to take up a second career and become trained as a science teacher. During my first dozen years teaching at Oakcrest School in Virginia, I wrote one prayer-poem for each graduating class. This is the first, dedicated to the class of 2012, and I often use one phrase from it as an aspiration. Here is the entire poem addressed to God:

To you I give my everything
with nothing left behind:
my heart, my soul, my body still,
in fact, my very mind,
which wanders through the past and possible,
seldom on present to dwell,
but I'm glad to say whose deepest recesses
only you can tell.

To you I leave my everything
within your doors to keep,

while I go over to work away
or off to bed to sleep.
For whatever task is now at hand,
**it's my heart I trust the least;**
**nearest to you I freely lock it up,**
**so on you my heart can feast.**

For only to love you was I made,
only your face to dwell upon;
restless it becomes when facing another,
anything else that will once be gone.
Passing away and away go my things,
and even my talents and dreams,
but there's something of this that
will endure through all time,
for eternal love eternally gleams.

Forever, forever seems an impossible word,
but I know it's your specialty, Lord.
Then make my forever, forever with you:
eternal love, eternally mine.

Another significant scene with St. John is at the foot of the Cross, when he's leaning on the strength of Mary. It is easier to ask for help when I stop considering myself as self-sufficient and I, instead, know not to trust myself alone. St. Josemaría wrote in *The Way of the Cross* about choosing to nail himself to the Cross of Christ: "I am yours and I give my whole self to You; gladly do I nail myself to the Cross, ready to be in the crossroads of this world a soul dedicated to You."[6] I think of that image often as I pray in front of the tabernacle about putting my trust in God alone; for without him, my heart would surely wander. I see myself as tethered to the Cross, and simultaneously to the tabernacle. To wander away from the latter surely means I am wandering away from the former—a risk I never want to take!

I have already referred to moments during my teenage years when I was especially doubtful of the value of apostolic celibacy. One retreat I made increased my trust in God on this point. I originally shared

6. Escrivá, *The Way of the Cross*, p. 71.

this rather dramatic story in another book and used a pseudonym for my classmate's name. I'd like to recount it again for you.

> Jack and I had been friends since fifth grade and in fact he took me on my first official date to the eighth-grade dance, when all the hairspray from my bangs ended up on his dress shirt after just one slow dance. By senior year of high school, our friendship had cooled a lot, especially after he "ruined" my fifteenth birthday party by getting pretty aggressive with one of my best friends, an effect of the anabolic steroids he had been taking to bulk himself up for football.
>
> During that senior year, I made my first five-day silent retreat over Christmas break, as part of my trying to take seriously a vocational call to apostolic celibacy in Opus Dei that I had repeatedly sensed over a two-year stint of intense prayer. The main theme of my retreat was my doubts about the value of following a vocation in the Church and especially about a call to celibacy (because I thought I had a

better plan for my life). A few days into the retreat, I perceived a very specific divine inspiration to pray for one of the boys in my American Studies class who was about to die. I even told a friend on the retreat so that she could also pray. I stayed on my knees a lot of the remainder of the retreat, but when I returned to school everyone was still alive and well. "It must have been my imagination," I concluded.

Our final project for American Studies was a presentation, during which Jack confessed to having gotten drunk twenty-five times during the month of December and having driven his car on twenty-one of those occasions, "wanting something bad to happen." This was Jack's response to his father having been diagnosed with cancer. Jack's presentation was a thank you to our teachers for having gotten him professional help and facilitating better communication with his parents, and also to his friends for having alerted the teachers. He didn't know to, or need to, thank me. In retrospect, I know that God saved Jack's life that Christmas. And I learned an important lesson for my own journey as an apostle: namely, that the immensity of the value of my vocation includes my getting to witness God save souls around me, that my prayer would facilitate others playing their part even when I was not the protagonist in helping someone, and that the first person God would draw closer to himself through my apostolate would always be me. God answered all my doubts on that retreat.[7]

---

7. Stephen Gabriel, *Put Out into the Deep: Become the Apostle You Are Called to Be* (New York: Scepter, 2024), pp. 73-75.

CHAPTER 7

# Being Around Noble Men

"Jack" was my first real date, but not my last. I grew up around brothers and other boys, and I was pretty boy-crazy by the beginning of high school. I dated someone seriously during my sophomore year (as "seriously" as one can at that age) while maintaining an obsession for an upperclassman athlete who wouldn't give me the time of day. That same year, I spent chemistry class trying to convince a "bad boy" to stop using alcohol, marijuana, and women. With hindsight, I realize how most of those attempts at converting bad boys end: with the good girl becoming corrupted rather than the bad boy being converted. If I had not worked part-time in a center of Opus

Dei, joining them for family gatherings and World Youth Day in that summer of 1993, I might easily have spent that summer in the front seat (or even the backseat) of the car belonging to any number of "bad boys." Idle summers during teen years can lead to big mistakes. As St. Josemaría said, "Satan and his allies never take a holiday."[1] I feel great shame in that reality, and recognize that the Lord saved me—not from a boy, but from myself.

I suppose this is logical, but it must be said: when someone commits to a life devoted to God through celibacy, hormones and pheromones continue their biological function. There have been weeks—even years—in which I have often chosen to stay home from social functions in order to entrust myself more to God and less to my own heart and will. If I feel weak against temptation, if my heart feels especially vulnerable, I lean upon the words: "It's my heart I trust the least. / With you, I freely lock it up, / so that on you it may feast." And also: "The Lord is my rock, and my fortress,

1. Josemaría Escrivá, *Friends of God* (Scepter: New York, 2002), no. 62.

and my deliverer, my God, my rock, in whom I take refuge, my shield, and the horn of my salvation, my stronghold" (Ps 18:2).

I have witnessed a one-hundred-percent survival rate of those men who, at some point in their youth, communicated by word, or deed, or song that they could not live without me: they all moved on once I made my intentions known! The diary of Mary Churchill recounts her learning the lesson that a girl does not have to marry the first man who falls in love with her.[2] Girls easily fall prey to pity for a young man, and their empathy and compassion often compel them to feel guilty about turning a good guy down. I discovered early on that it is actually cruel to provide mixed messages to a boy, and compassionate to simply and clearly set him free. My honesty is giving him the freedom to live out his own vocation.

Luckily, most men whom I have been surrounded with as an adult have been honorable and trustworthy:

2. Erik Larson, *The Splendid and the Vile: A Saga of Churchill, Family, and Defiance During the Blitz* (New York: Crown Publishing Group, 2020), p. 478.

men who could be considered greathearted and noble. They have therefore become sources of inspiration rather than temptation. I consider my own fidelity to celibacy, in part, as a faithfulness to them too. Being steadfast in my own vocation is an encouraging way to be accountable to each other.

Fidelity to my celibacy is something I must renew each day, just as a promise to the sacrament of marriage is renewed in thought, word, and action each day. I repeatedly offer to God my sexuality: all that I am just as he made me, no matter my thoughts or feelings, strengths or weaknesses that day. I look back at the years of my repeated renewal from the vantage point of thirty years of daily self-offering to the Lord and see clearly how God has made my offering fruitful. Just as a mutual gift of self bears incredible fruit in a marriage, so does my self-gift to God, who in turn is able to work through me to bring about great fruitfulness. It's been up to him how he bears fruit, in my life just as in any woman's life.

This brings me to a question I'm often asked concerning men and apostolic celibacy: how is apostolic celibacy the same and how is it different for women than it is for men? In his book *Why Celibacy: Reclaiming the Fatherhood of the Priest*, Fr. Carter Griffin refers to the Fathers of the Church when discussing the paternal fruitfulness of Christ. "As the New Adam, he is betrothed to the New Eve, represented by Mary and fulfilled in his Bride the Church, born, as the Fathers often say, from his side on the Cross."[3] Christ is therefore the origin and model for all celibate vocations, both men and women. The life-bearing sacrifice of Our Lord is on a much higher plane than human reproduction, so what is most fundamental in a man's or a woman's identification with Christ in following a call to celibacy is the same.

The differences between men and women are based on the the very real physical and psychological complementarity between the sexes (which is its own topic for a different book). Women's libidos rise and fall and reach their height in the early- to mid-forties. Not only do experiences of sexual drives and hormones differ among various women living out this celibate calling, but they

3. Griffin, pp. 6–7.

differ greatly throughout one woman's life as she strives to live celibacy faithfully. My self-offering is an integral and cohesive offering of everything that I am as a woman—mind, body, and spirit. An intricate part of being a woman is the identity of being a life-bearer. Men, in their apostolic celibacy, are likewise living out the particular calling to all men: to be givers of God's life and love.

A woman's healthy reproductive system is for far more than sexual intercourse: her body is also receptive and life-bearing. In relation to God's calling to live a life of celibacy, I value the witness of my fellow life-bearers, of holy women whose legacies include happy marriages and families, for we are all called to a special and particular fruitfulness. Luckily, I have no shortage of such examples in my life.

Surrounding myself with great women is also pivotal to my apostolic celibacy! The qualities of many inspiring women could be long enough topics for another book, but particularly I think of Bl. Guadalupe Ortiz de Landázuri's life and letters, which provide ample examples of generous availability, fruitful apostolic endeavors, daring professional projects, and sincere friendship.[4] I have known, lived with, and met many such women.

When I was twenty-seven years old, two of my closest friends, also my age, separately confided in me that they wanted to have a baby. Even if they were not yet in love with a man, they could *feel* the desire in their bodies and in their hearts. Indeed, I was experiencing the same thing. We concluded that what we were all experiencing was hormonal, encountering similar desires in the same period of our lives. But this was also an encounter with our feminine genius, a calling put into our hearts by God, and his way of communicating to each of us uniquely and individually. In fact, we were all called to motherhood, and we all eventually responded affirmatively to this calling, albeit in different ways.

For a woman to respond affirmatively to God's invitation to apostolic celibacy, it is crucial for her to understand what it means to offer her entire self,

4. See Cristina Abad Cadenas, *Guadalupe: The Freedom of Loving* (New York: Scepter, 2018). Also see Mercedes Eguíbar Galarza, *Blessed Guadalupe Ortiz de Landázuri* (Milan: Edicione Ares, 2019).

including her sexuality, to God so that he can bear fruit through her life. In offering my sexuality to God, he gave me a beautiful motherhood in return. The history of the Church, of which Opus Dei's history is part and parcel, attests to the reality of spiritual motherhood and its spiritual fruit, through which many marriages and families are brought closer to God. My motherhood is the act of being a conduit of God's love in this world, which bears its own eternal fruit.

Of the three of us friends who were once twenty-seven years old together, I am living apostolic celibacy, and the other two entered into the sacrament of marriage. One friend said yes to God by lovingly bearing and rearing her own children. The other said yes to God by raising several children whom she and her husband adopted since they could not conceive. God works wonders through the life-giving capacity of a woman, even when he asks for the very real sacrifice not to bear her own children.

The model *par excellence* of a woman being open to God's perfect plan is Our Lady, mysteriously both virgin and mother. Mary lived a life of celibacy and at the same time made her womb available to the action of the Holy Spirit. Indeed, she is a perfect model for us all, and her life, her *fiat*, and her motherhood are all mysteries worth pondering and imitating in our own lives. Mary brings us by the hand into the mysteries of God.

Here is another poem I wrote that I return to often as a way to depend more and more on Mary's motherly help:

Into the banquet I am bidden—
To the conference, led by her hand.
To his intimacies I have no right,
but as his daughter, I just might
catch a phrase that he has spoken,
hear of a promise never broken,
know of his love that fills the room,
love in his knowing, now and soon.

My little soul cannot contain,
nor comprehend my little brain,
but when he dwells inside of me,
taken up I seem to be.

Into the banquet I am bidden—
to the conference, led by her hand.
Though so much still lies from me hidden,
now I cannot but understand.

CHAPTER 8

# Being a Lover Who Bears Fruit

A common fear for women considering celibacy is that of ending up being physically and spiritually barren, of bearing no fruit in this world. And yet, a woman's life-giving capacity comes in many forms. "Life-giving love" is one way to describe the spread of the Gospel and the universal call to holiness. We live love when we open people's eyes to God's love and the gift of being with him for eternity. Our Christian mission, starting with our baptism, can be summarized as loving and serving Christ with one's whole heart, mind, soul, and body, and serving others for God's sake.

A lifetime of interplay between God's will and the Christian's freedom is what often gets referred to with the term *vocation*—as in a vocation to the religious life, to marriage, or to apostolic celibacy. These are specific paths in which the whole person encounters, listens to, talks to, and follows Christ.

These paths often take twists and turns, even in the life of a very happy disciple. Sometimes, these twists and turns include God presenting a new and different path altogether. This might occur if someone recognizes that her more fundamental divine vocation to be happy and holy is not being fulfilled in the specified path of celibacy. Ideally, this recognition comes during the time created for discernment, like an engagement period, which in Opus Dei consists of a minimum of five years. Among my many friends who are now happily married, I can identify some who were engaged to a different man from their husbands, and there are others who spent some time generously living as celibate members of Opus Dei. No vows were broken in any case; the commitment in Opus Dei never involves vows anyhow. If a person arrives at this difficult discernment, they will set their new path toward God, and God will, of course, never stop calling that person to himself with guidance and grace. It is paramount that everyone in the Church support each other through these twists and turns and recognize the enormous difference between a detour in vocation led by the Lord and a turning away from the Lord.

In the case, then, of a woman who happily continues on the specific path of apostolic celibacy, the fundamental calling to life-giving love is always fulfilled by God. It is he who created us with the fundamental desire to give and receive love, and so it is logical that, if he calls a person to celibacy, he would fully satisfy that person's heart, made for love, through his own love. For the sake of simplicity, let's use the term *apostolic fruit* for the myriad of blessings that come from the life-giving love of a celibate Christian.

About a year ago, I was complaining to God in my prayer—which I admit I do far too often!—about the lack of visible results in my apostolic work. I quickly had the sense of being reprimanded—by my conscience, or guardian angel, or the Lord himself, I do not know. But what I do know was that God was reminding me that he did not need to show me any fruits at all, and that I needed to trust and believe even without seeing. I was reprimanded just as St. Thomas was: "Blessed are those who have not seen and yet believe" (Jn 20:29). I resolved to pray often something like this: "God, you do not need to show me any fruits at all in order to win my loyalty. I'm trying to be faithful to you alone. But, if you show me any fruits, I'll happily take any and all of them to bolster me along my way."

God inspired me to focus on the idea that the fruit of holy lives lived well until they are called to depart this earth is the chief apostolic fruit for me to behold. And if I failed to recognize even those holy lives around me, then I was missing the point of my life of celibacy: namely, the salvation of souls. I mentioned earlier that my mother died when I was twenty-two years old. She was well known for her holiness, lived in cheerfulness and simplicity. I have lived with quite a few earthly saints since I left my parents' home, many of whom were called to their heavenly abode. I have come to find comfort and peace in attending funerals, particularly those of older women who were members of Opus Dei. During these holy moments of memory and loss, numerous profound stories are recounted of the many people whose lives they've touched. Married women invariably leave indelible marks of God's love on their family members, and often there are many grandchildren whose lives are a testament to the love that was perpetuated throughout the generations.

Women who lived their lives in apostolic celibacy likewise have inspiring stories told of them, stories of virtue and heroism often suitable for history books. The apostolic fruit from celibacy always includes, even when we cannot see it, the reality that God brings souls closer to himself through one's life. Spiritual motherhood implies spiritual children and grandchildren. The family unit, seen in Christmas cards and written down in family trees, is not visually represented when one's parenthood is spiritual in nature, and so it is an act of faith to place one's security in God's ability to bear fruit in one's life. A wise priest named Fr. Ron Gillis, who at the time was chaplain of Oakcrest School, once told me in response to my doubts of God's promise of fruitfulness in my life that "we raise whole families."

He told me that he had seen this reality in his own life and that I would be blessed to witness it one day, too. Even as Jesus reprimanded Thomas for his unbelief, he still blessed his life with palpable representations of the fruitfulness of his labor for Christ. Fr. Gillis received the same reassurance in the fruits of his faithfulness: he saw himself as a grandparent of families. I have indeed seen the fruits of the spiritual motherhood lived by celibate members of Opus Dei already in my lifetime—even though I'm barely the age of the youngest-possible grandparent! God indeed is good!

What's more, I have never felt that I have sacrificed family life for the sake of apostolic celibacy, since I have always lived in Opus Dei centers, which are true family homes. My family life is fruitful, loving, and life-giving. My first time living in an Opus Dei center (as a college student), I was struck by the beauty of the new family God had given me. I recall taking a moment to look around during a house gathering and realizing how miraculous it was that I was surrounded by women who were living together with the united desire to love and please God.

The pluralism within any center of Opus Dei is inspiring, often displaying a blend of generations, diverse ethnic and cultural backgrounds, various personalities, and differing opinions on debatable issues. Just as in any family, people can push each other's buttons, even though we are all adults and all aspiring to be better versions of ourselves. A group of unrelated women, from all types of experiences and backgrounds, living together as a family with God as their head, is a Christian witness in and of itself. It's a witness for outsiders to see our unity amidst diversity: Jesus is the great unifier, our Lord in the Blessed Sacrament present in our centers. It is not at all the case that we get along because we are all trying to be good. Rather, Our Lord's presence in the Tabernacle helps each of us to increasingly see other people the way he sees them. Our unity amidst diversity also attests to the reality that God bears fruit in our lives by gathering us into a family, united in spiritual aims, as children of a spiritual father, namely St. Josemaría. The family aspect is itself one of the most visible fruits of our apostolic celibacy.

I share with you a poem I wrote about loving others as the Lord desires:

I have no need of new intents
to love You, Lord, but I lament
the need I have to start again
each time I lack with human kin
the sacrificial form of love
that should move me to place You above,
and should You in others find.

But, lo, I am still so blind! so blind!
to the divine within each soul:
the close, the far, the good, the foul;
all deserve the best from me. Then grant
me, Lord, more of Your life,
more of Your love, more of Your grace,
so I may see them from Thy face,
that I may hear them with Your ears,
and take them in with Your embrace.

Alone I only shy away—
so, wash my ego with Your tears,
so mine can wash them, with no fear.

CHAPTER 9

# Being at the Doorway to Heaven

In 2002, when John Paul II introduced the Luminous Mysteries of the Rosary to the world, a married friend of mine shared with me how happy she was to have a conduit to regularly contemplate the mystery of her own vocation. I decided then and there that I also wanted to dedicate a particular mystery of the Rosary to the contemplation of my own path. I settled on the fourth Luminous Mystery, the scene of the Transfiguration, as appropriate for apostolic celibacy: the three witnesses of the event—Peter, James, and John—experienced a foretaste of heaven, with all their five senses engaged, while their feet were firmly planted on the earth. This spoke to my particular experience of the gift God had offered to me in apostolic celibacy. In the Eucharist, heaven is thinly veiled for all Catholics. For those of us living apostolic celibacy, reception of the Eucharist should have a more poignant significance, since our whole selves, including our bodies, have been dedicated to the Lord in service of the Church. The Lord invited me, mind, body, and soul, to be his witness, just as he invited his three apostles. I try to recall the beauty of this invitation while participating in Mass and Eucharistic Benediction.

When I attend Mass, I purposely do some "heavy lifting," which entails carrying all the weightiest matters of my soul to the altar. I bring with me the needs of the whole world in addition to my own personal frustrations. To show him that he is truly my best friend, I try to be a channel by which he can carry out his intentions for the day. I gather all those needs and intentions together, imagining that I lift them as high as I can overhead, allowing God to then draw them up, just out of my reach, so that he can hold all those weighty issues for me while I pray peacefully, sensing that his sharing the burden with me eases my yoke.

During Mass, we touch eternity. All the frustrations and intentions look different from an eternal perspective, from God's vantage point. God resolves each problem much more effectively than we ever could, no matter how hard we work or how much we worry.

All Catholics can, and must, carry their own intentions to the altar at the offertory of Mass. Any Catholic can experience the ease of the yoke that is taken on by Christ himself at the Holy Sacrifice. We all anticipate full communion with God one day in body and soul; and yet, those living apostolic celibacy lead others in the anticipation of total union with God, body and soul, through our witness of celibacy. And so, we experience a special yearning for communion with God that is complete. This heavenly communion that celibacy represents involves our will (wanting God's will even when that is uncertain) and our body (yearning for the resurrection of the body).

Receiving the Eucharist is like standing at the doorway to heaven. This realization makes me want to celebrate in heart, mind, and body—to kneel and to sing—bodily gestures that correspond to the unseen reality present through the doorway.

# EPILOGUE

The summer that God chose me is the summer that I chose God. Looking back at my journey from my current vantage point exactly thirty years later, I start to cry as I consider how easily I could have thrown away the beautiful gift that God offered me in apostolic celibacy. There are countless moments when I could have walked away. I hope that these chapters have conveyed some of my gratitude to those who have helped me along the way. I am grateful for those who have come before me, and I pray for those who walk this journey with me and for those who will come after me, with the resounding acclamation I share with St. Josemaría: "Love . . . is well worth any love!"[1]

1. Escrivá, *The Way*, no. 171.

Your life and love deserve a place in
each and every heart.
Yet, when I look out upon the world,
I ask: where should I start?

So many souls yearn for truth,
and thirst for joy that lasts.
But they don't know what or where
to find the fount so vast.

How much I pity those who have not
kissed your hands and side,
and have not kissed you with their mouths
and thus, brought you inside.

Burn a hot fire inside my heart
that purifies all there,
so, I can love every soul,
but with the Love you bear.

Zealous were the saints for souls,
eager to gain friends.

Make saints for a world in dire need,
until the world ends.

Angela Therese Fortunato
April 5, 2024

# FURTHER READING


Benedict XVI. (December 22, 2006) *Address to the Roman Curia.*

———. (2007) *Jesus of Nazareth: From the Baptism in the Jordan to the Transfiguration.* New York: Doubleday.

Buch, Lucas. (2020) *Divine Insights: St. Josemaría's New Mediterraneans.* New York: Scepter.

Read chapter 3, "From the Wound of the Right Hand."

Escrivá, Josemaría. (2002) *The Way of the Cross.* New York: Scepter.

———. (2002) *Christ is Passing By.* New York: Scepter.

———. (2002) *Friends of God.* New York: Scepter.

———. (2007) *Conversations with Saint Josemaría Escrivá.* New York: Scepter.

———. (2010) *The Way*. New York: Scepter.

Gabriel, Stephen. (2024) *Put Out into the Deep: Become the Apostle You Are Called to Be*. New York: Scepter.

Giesler, Michael E. (January 2009) "Celibacy in the First Two Centuries." *Homiletic and Pastoral Review*. Celibacy-in-the-first-Centuries.pdf, www.fathersofthechurch.com.

Guardini, Romano. (1954) *The Lord*. Chicago: Henry Regnery Company.

Read chapter "Christian Marriage and Virginity."

Griffin, Carter. (2019) *Why Celibacy: Reclaiming the Fatherhood of the Priest*. Steubenville, Ohio: Emmaus Road Publishing.

John Paul II. (2006) *Man and Woman He Created Them: A Theology of the Body*. Boston, MA: Daughters of St. Paul.

Read 1:1 "The Meaning of Original Unity"; 1:3 "Continence for the Kingdom of Heaven"; 2:1 "Ephesians 5:21–33."

Larson, Erik. (2020) *The Splendid and the Vile*. New York: Crown.

León, Borja de, ed. (2021) *He Calls, We Answer: St. Josemaría on Vocation*. New York: Scepter.

Read chapter 6, "Giving Our Lives for Our Friends."

Leonardi Mauro. (2011) *Come Gesù: L'amicizia e il dono del celibato apostolico libro*. Maggio: Ares.

McGovern, Thomas. (2002) *Priestly Identity: A Study in the Theology of the Priesthood*. Dublin: Four Courts Press.

Newman, John Henry. (1869) *Parochial and Plain Sermons*, vol. 2. London: Rivingtons.

Read sermon 5, "Love of Relations and Friends."

Opus Dei. (February 23, 2016) "Members of Opus Dei." https://opusdei.org/en-us/article/membersof-opus-dei/.

———. (September 28, 2023) "Apostles Who Give Life." https://opusdei.org/en/article/apostles-who-give-life/.

Weigel, George. (2022) *To Sanctify the World: The Vital Legacy of Vatican II*. New York: Basic Books.

# ACKNOWLEDGMENTS

St. Josemaría often said that ninety percent of someone's vocation could be attributed to their parents. That is certainly true in my case, and I first want to acknowledge my parents. I have received sufficient assurance from Our Lord that they are both enjoying their heavenly reward, and that moves me even more to pray for them with filial gratitude. I also pray to them for many intentions, especially those pertaining to my siblings, two nephews, and two nieces. I like to say that my father was a supernumerary and my mother was a saint, and I can see my dad give his big smile and chuckle in agreement with that summary. My mother was a cooperator of Opus Dei, which means that she was never a member and did not receive the calling to join Opus Dei. She supported its apostolic work in many ways, including spreading devotion to the founder, St. Josemaría, by mailing his prayer card to almost every person she knew when she was ill . . . and, of course, by supporting two of her children in our vocation as numerary members.

As a faith-filled professor, wife, and mother, my sister continues to be a role model for me. I would certainly not be who I am without my three brothers, and I try not to let on just how much I admire each of them. We recently discussed how our family culture growing up included our father's nerdy interest in *Star Trek*. As high school kids, we usually went out only after watching *Star Trek: The Next Generation* together with my dad. Fortunato family culture also included performing songs and dances, including Filipino folk dances that my mother taught my younger brother and me. I fondly recall one Mother's Day when we kids sang her "Teach Your Children" by Crosby, Stills, Nash & Young with some homemade instruments. I also recall my mother reciting her original acrostic poem forming the word "cherish" to my grandmother, who lived with us for many years. I want to thank my entire extended family on both the Italian-American and Filipino sides, even though I don't have space here for cousins, aunts, and uncles. Thanks for all the great memories!

I would also like to acknowledge the great help I received on this little project of mine. *Wholeheartedly* would not have made it to the printed page without the encouragement and input from Dia Boyle, Steve Gabriel, Helen Keefe, Rebekah Chin Lee, Rosalie Stoner, Ann Marie Klein, Fr. Peter Armenio, Julie Barder, Josephina Ouyang, and of course the Scepter team, especially Mike Aquilina and Meredith Koopman.

Finally, I cannot say enough about the many, many holy women I have been privileged to know in Opus Dei, and particularly those living apostolic celibacy. You know who you are. You are so accustomed to being in the background and to hardly ever being thanked. Maybe you're too accustomed to never being thanked. So, thank you!